LITTLE LIBRARY

Guide to
Italy

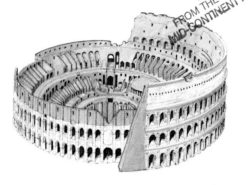

Simon Buckland

Kingfisher Books

NEW YORK

Contents

Welcome to Italy

The road winds steeply uphill between groves of olive trees. At the top, old houses with tiled roofs are grouped around the tall tower of a church. You are in a Tuscan hill town in the heart of Italy.

Exploring old towns is just one of the ways to enjoy a visit to Italy. You are about to discover many others!

Italy and its islands

Italy is a long and thin country sticking out into the sea. People often say that it looks like a boot! The snowy Alps divide Italy from the rest of Europe. More mountains, the Apennines, run like a spine down the middle. Most of Italy is within 60 miles of the coast, and there are lots of lovely beaches. There are also two big islands — Sicily and Sardinia.

ITALIAN MONEY

In Italy, the money people use is called lire — both coins and notes. When you go to a bank, you'll see signs showing how much Italian money you can get in exchange for your own money.

Czech Republic

Germany

Austria

Hungary

Switzerland

ALPS

Slovenia

Croatia

Milan

ALPS

Venice

R. Po

Florence

Pisa

Corsica
(France)

R. Tiber

Adriatic Sea

Rome

ITALY

Bari

Naples

Sardinia

MEDITERRANEAN
SEA

Sicily

In a town square

Most Italian towns and villages have a main square, called the *piazza*, often with an old church to one side or nearby. You'll also find cafés, restaurants, and stores — the *piazza* is usually the busiest place in town! It's a good place to meet friends, have a cool drink, or just watch what's going on.

① Drugstore
② Bakery
③ Pizzeria
④ Bank
⑤ Delicatessen
⑥ Ice cream shop
⑦ Fruit store

AT THE GELATERIA

Italy is famous for its *gelati* (ice cream), and was probably the first place in Europe to make it. There are lots of wonderful flavors — even the cones are delicious! You might like to try *cioccolato* (chocolate), *fragola* (strawberry), *nocciola* (hazelnut), *torrone* (nougat), *limone* (lemon).

Going shopping

Shopping in Italy can be great fun, especially if you're buying food. Most Italians buy it fresh each day from market stalls or from small stores like this *salumeria*, which sells cooked meat, salads, and cheeses. Shops usually close for about three hours in the middle of the day, but then reopen until about 8 P.M. Many close on Monday, as well as all day on Sunday.

orologio
(watch)

occhiali da sole
(sunglasses)

berretto
(cap)

costume da bagno
(swimsuit)

You won't have a problem if you forget your favorite T-shirt — the stores are packed with marvelous clothes.

11

In a trattoria

I talians enjoy eating out and many families go to a trattoria every Sunday for lunch. They're good places to try local food. You should be able to order pizza – it was invented in Naples, in the south, 200 years ago. Each trattoria will also have its own special dishes, known as *specialità della casa*.

MAKE A PIZZA

Here's a quick and easy recipe for pizza. Ask a grown-up to help you with the oven.

1½ cups self-rising flour
4 tbsp. margarine
⅔ cups milk
½ tsp. salt
Tomato paste

1 Sift the flour and salt into a mixing bowl, then rub in the margarine.
2 When the mixture looks like bread–crumbs, add the milk and mix to make a soft dough.
3 Roll the pizza dough out into a circle. Put it on a greased baking tray.
4 Spread your pizza base with tomato paste, then top with slices of cheese.

5 Add your favorite toppings — olives, mushrooms, pepperoni, peppers, sausage, anchovies. Sprinkle with herbs.
6 Bake at 425°F for 20 to 25 minutes.

Eating and drinking

Wherever you go in Italy, you'll find pasta on the menu. Most Italians eat it every day, usually before a main course of meat or fish. People often have wine with meals and they also drink a lot of strong coffee. You might like to try a delicious cool drink, such as *granita di lemone* — made from lemons and crushed ice.

Appetizers are called *antipasti*. As well as olives and vegetables, there may be slices of salami or ham (*prosciutto*).

Then there's pasta, with all sorts of different sauces. *Spaghetti alla Napoletana* is a tomato sauce, *carbonara* is with bacon and eggs.

ALL SORTS OF PASTA

Pasta comes in all shapes and sizes in Italy — there are over 500 different kinds! Often the name for a kind of pasta comes from its shape. *Conchiglie* means seashell, for example, while *farfalle* means butterfly.

Penne

Fusilli

Conchiglie

Ravioli

Farfalle

A fish or meat course comes next, and it's usually eaten with a fresh salad. Fish is called *pesce* and *alla griglia* means grilled.

If you're still hungry you can have a dessert (*dolce*), fresh fruit, or cheese (*formaggio*).

Things to see and do

Italy is a place where you can travel back into the past. At least that's what it can feel like when you visit the lovely old towns and cities. Sightseers' favorites are Florence, Rome, and the island city of Venice — all with museums and churches packed full of beautiful works of art. Then there's Pisa with its famous tower and the ancient Roman town of Pompeii, near Naples.

Traditional boats, called gondolas, are a fun way to travel around Venice's waterways.

Pisa's Leaning Tower wasn't always crooked — it's been sinking into the ground since it was built more than 800 years ago.

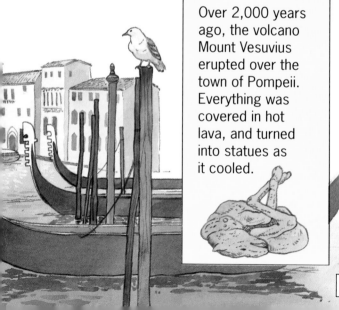

Over 2,000 years ago, the volcano Mount Vesuvius erupted over the town of Pompeii. Everything was covered in hot lava, and turned into statues as it cooled.

A visit to Rome

About 2,000 years ago, the city of Rome was the center of a great empire which stretched over the whole of Europe. Today, it is the capital of Italy and the home of the pope.

The many wonderful old buildings in Rome include the huge circular Colosseum, shown below. It was here that ancient Romans watched deadly fights between men called gladiators and wild animals such as lions, elephants, and tigers.

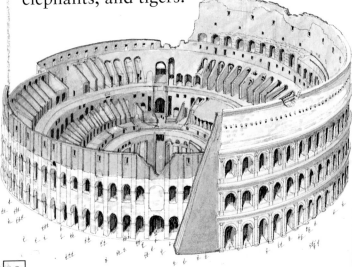

Rome is an exciting mixture of the past and the present. As well as amazing old buildings, such as churches, museums, and art galleries, there are also modern offices, stores, and new cafés and restaurants.

ST. PETER'S

The pope lives in a city of his own called the Vatican, inside Rome. St. Peter's is the Vatican's main church. Several times a year, huge crowds gather to be blessed by the pope.

Traveling around

If you are exploring a busy city, it's best to walk or go by bus — or you can use subway trains when you are in Rome or Milan.

Outside the cities, a car is a good way to tour around. For very long trips, express trains and planes are quickest. To cross from the mainland to an island, you can take a car ferry or a hydrofoil (*aliscafo*), like the one shown below.

Highways are called *autostrade*. Spectacular bridges cut through the mountains.

BICYCLING

Italians are enthusiastic cyclists, and you may see people racing on weekends. The weather gets too hot, and the roads too busy for cycling vacations, though.

Sports and games

Soccer is enormously popular in Italy. You'll see people playing it everywhere you go, while town and city stadiums are crowded with fans on Sunday afternoons during the season. The best-known teams are Juventus of Turin, Inter-Milan, and Roma (Rome).

Motor racing is another favorite sport. The Italian Grand Prix is held at the Monza circuit in the city of Milan.

Italy has plenty of beautiful sandy beaches. The warm, clear seawater is great for swimming. Scuba diving and snorkeling are popular, too.

△ The *Palio* is a horse race which takes place every July and August in the streets of Siena, south of Florence.

▽ Many of the world's top soccer players play for Italian teams. Soccer is called *calcio*, and *stadio* means stadium.

School and holidays

Italian students have to go to school every morning except Sunday, but lessons finish at lunchtime! There are quite long vacations too — two months during the summer, and a whole month at Christmas time.

Older students have to do some homework in the afternoon, but younger ones can spend their free time playing games.

AN ITALIAN PLAYGROUND GAME

This Italian game is just like "Ring-around-a-rosy." Sing and spin around quickly until you all fall down. The words are:

Gira gira tondo,
Casca il mondo,
Casca la terra,
Tutti giù per terra!

This means:
Round and round,
Down falls the earth,
Down falls the ground,
All fall down!

CONFETTI

Confetti are small sugared almonds given to friends and relatives on special days. White ones are given to people when they get married.

Celebrations

Nearly every town in Italy has a spectacular carnival each year, with colorful street processions and fireworks. There are puppet shows, too.

People dress up in special costumes at carnival time, and many of them wear beautiful masks.

MAKE A CARNIVAL MASK

You'll need a pencil, some cardboard, scissors, silver paint, glue, colorful glitter, tape, and a thin stick (about 10 in. long).

1 Draw a mask on the cardboard and cut it out. Hold it to your face and ask someone to mark where your eyes are. Cut out eye holes.

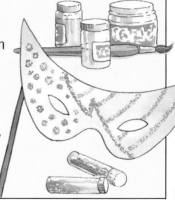

2 Paint your mask silver and leave it until it's completely dry.
3 Cover it with a thin layer of glue, then sprinkle on some of the colored glitter, making patterns.
4 To make a handle, tape the stick to one side of your mask.

◁ The wildest carnival masks and costumes are worn by the people of Venice. At this carnival, people eat a special treat called *frittelle* (apple fritters).

27

Let's speak Italian!

NUMBERS

1	*Uno*
2	*Due*
3	*Tre*
4	*Quattro*
5	*Cinque*
6	*Sei*
7	*Sette*
8	*Otto*
9	*Nove*
10	*Dieci*

Buon giorno
Hello

Per favore
Please

Grazie
Thank you

Vorrei un gelato, per favore.
I'd like some ice cream, please.
Questo, quant'è?
How much is this one?

Parla inglese?
Do you speak English?

No
No

Sì
Yes

Index